L'dor Vador
לדור ודור
From Generation to Generation

poems by

Steve Pollack

Finishing Line Press
Georgetown, Kentucky

*Tell your children about it
and let your children tell theirs,
and their children the next generation!*

Book of Joel (Yoel) 1:3

L'dor Vador
לדור ודור
From Generation to Generation

*For grandparents, parents
aunts, uncles
sister & cousins
children & grandchildren,
ancestors who I did not meet
generations who will not meet me.*

These are your stories, too.

*Linda, my first listener
often my subject, forever my love
your tender face tells me
all I need.*

Copyright © 2020 by Steve Pollack
ISBN 978-1-64662-230-6 First Edition
All rights reserved under International and Pan-American Copyright Conventions.
No part of this book may be reproduced in any manner whatsoever without written permission from the publisher, except in the case of brief quotations embodied in critical articles and reviews.

ACKNOWLEDGMENTS

With grateful appreciation, I acknowledge print anthologies and web journals, where the following poems first appeared. These publications encouraged more poems, and this book, where poems talk to each other:

Schuylkill Valley Journal: "L'dor Vador"
Poetica Magazine: "Poppy;" "Prayer" (as, "What Touches a Human Heart")
Zingara Review: "Chaninah"
Copperfield Review: "Here I Am;" "Gettysburg"
The Write Place at the Write Time: "Roots"
Moonstone Art Center—*Yearning to Breath Free: Poetry from the Immigrant Community*: "Letter to Miss Liberty"

Kind people from Tasmania to Kentucky first read my words in cyberspace, lauching an improbable and deeply satisfying journey. Sharing a curious drive to write poems, to love the craft, comforts a task often lonely. Around Philly, I met fellow poets too numerous to name, at readings and open mics; a diverse, welcoming community. At the *Mad Poets Critique Circle* in Wallingford, led by Amy Laub with a firm, and light touch—feedback and exposure to dozens more poems, sharpened my work. Closer to home, at the Indian Valley Public Library, friends circle on first Saturdays. I cheer the *Forgotten Voices* poetry group founded by Joanne Leva—you inspire us with your energy & love. Thank you also, Amy Small-McKinney, a guide through tangled forests of lines and stanzas, to that clearing where poems open to sky.

Publisher: Leah Maines
Editor: Christen Kincaid
Cover Art: Cathleen Cohen, cathleencohenart.com
Author Photo: Scott Beadenkopf, fscott.smugmug.com
Cover Design: Elizabeth Maines McCleavy

Printed in the USA on acid-free paper.
Order online: www.finishinglinepress.com
        also available on amazon.com

Author inquiries and mail orders:
Finishing Line Press
P. O. Box 1626
Georgetown, Kentucky 40324
U. S. A.

Table of Contents

L'dor Vador 1
Poppy 2
Sophie 3
1521 Dickinson Street 4
Anna 5
Chanina 6
Here I Am 7
roots 8
Ode to a Peach Tree on Oakland Street 9
Together 10
Unfenced Evenings 11
December 26, 1960 12
A Time to Every Purpose 13
Coming of Age 14
Bashert 15
Firstborn 16
Brothers 17
Gettysburg 18
Archaeology 19
Letter to Miss Liberty 20
Why the Oceans are Salty 21
Believe 22
Knock Knock 23
Lost and Found 24
What Would You Write? 26
For Your Sore Throat 27
Fairy Dust 28
How Do I Know You? 29
Guessing Game 30
Prayer 31
De Lorean Flight 32
Notes 33

L'dor Vador

Of four grandparents, three hugged me.
We walked to the corner candy store, rode
trolleys to meet a Yiddish-speaking parrot,
watched *Taras Bulba* in a darkened theatre.
Two grandparents swelled at my *bar-mitzvah*,
ten years later one lit a candle at my wedding.
None counted toes of great-grandchildren.

Assimilation, my grandparents rosy cure
being American their ironic dream.
A *shande* to talk about countries fled,
centuries of ancestors' bones
left buried, kin left behind
who never boarded a boat,
glass shattered, *shtetls* burned.

My grandchildren watch Jedi not Cossacks,
ride mini-vans not trolleys. Running to us
in contagious welcome, they call out:
"Bubbie, Zayda!" Too young to grasp
origins, too innocent to hold prejudice
their little arms, tight at our waists
wrap around generations who begot us.

My life is salted, *shmaltzed* by a world
gone, customs saved over waves. We fast
or feast by the same lunar calendar,
chant the same ancient words, faith
not estate bequeathed. Missing the hush
of Yiddish lullabies, a severed chain
of stories untold, questions unasked.

My first language English, attire modern,
desires American. Vanity is satisfied
by simple facts, my confession is not.
I want to know of simple strengths,
bleached beginnings. Which of Israel's
twelve wandering tribes, which mother
carried my seed, concubine or wife?

Poppy

When our best efforts were coming apart
at the seams, life's fabric wrinkled,
his voice soothed: *Everything will press out.*

His eyes smiling, head erect
backbone vested in thimbled sense
uncommon insights.
He made us believe.

Fitted with cap and gown,
star spangled opportunities unbuttoned
before us. Why should we feel like rags
torn by troubles, sorry for ourselves?

We were not suffocated by edicts
compelled by cruel persecution
to flee our homes. We did not fear mobs,
the Czar's army or Siberian winter.

Poppy held a sharp scissors
in his right hand every day,
cut tattered edges, loose threads.
He knew the measure of sacrifice.

Since he reached this *golden land*
alone,
sleeved in faith, trimmed
like optimism in satin resolve,

we are counting generations,
human stitches in the unfinished tapestry
his journey began.

There are cold places, threatening
as Siberian winter, each day uncertain
against hatred unzipped.

Don't worry! Unfold your hope,
mark these words of a humble tailor:
Everything will press out.

Sophie

We did not hold hands or play
wooden spools in the storefront.
I never heard your voice
or called you *Bubbe*.

Neither did you *kvell*
pleasure from my presence,
except to smooth hands over
your daughter's expectant bump.

Before newborn lungs filled
death stole your final breath.
From an oval frame, umber eyes
search the matching iris of my eyes.

You speak stilled in seamstress fashion
V-neck lace on vintage silk,
round locket below soft round face,
dense black braids elegantly up.

I speak the covenant scribed in flesh
on my eighth day, since that day
your name and mine—*Shprintze, Peretz*
threaded together by three Hebrew letters.

1521 Dickinson Street

Customers enter the shop in the middle of the block, garments in hand. Neighbors or strangers view the square South Philly face, on their way to the corner grocery, to tart lemon ice scooped from tin tubs or to pizza and pitcher at Strolli's. Aphrodisiacs served with mandolin music. Uncle Jake & Dad stride across asphalt, home from war, stars on storefront glass. Ready for fights on a twelve-inch tube. Mom turns north onto Broad Street, a pretty young girl with pressed habits for nuns at St. Rita's on Friday afternoons. Skipping home with cash and compliments.

Inside, Poppy bent at the familiar Singer, near a front counter. Mom's parents live in rooms behind steam, siblings on upper floors. Three older cousins, who also lived there remember shapes & finishes, local characters & kids, racks where we played or hid. The fire, overwhelmed by kindness. Four years after Bubbe Sophie passed, my sister delivered from Mt. Sinai at 4th and Reed. Change came as new houses sprouted in rows like bumper crops. Poppy and his sewing machine moved twelve miles Northeast with his youngest daughter's kosher family.

Shop sold, shuttered and silent. I hear hubbub. Details blurred, stories not made up—repeated around kitchen tables, imprinted black & white like scalloped snapshots at an age before memory: *marble steps scrubbed clean, worn smooth; lapels wide as city sidewalks.* Beginnings learned after endings— like my birth, nine months plus two weeks after Dad's army discharge, a document found in a box of pictures sixty-four years later, days after the date on his death certificate.

Before voices became digits on hand-held screens—before true and false argued as if they both know everything, I heard English, and Yiddish, and Italian, accents like cacciatore or tzimmes simmering on stovetops. I witnessed a cast iron machine treadled by feet, the needle wheeled up or down by hand. A place crowded with neccessity & love.

Now, reverent visitors peer at an artifact, idle behind museum plexiglass. An immigrant's livelihood. I watched my grandfather work with wool and cotton. The machine branded *Singer*, gifted by aged siblings. A plastic plaque on the rough walnut top, where Poppy labored, names Mazers and Franks and Pollacks—owners and donors—year not address—history short on story.

Anna

She chopped & mixed from scratch,
in wooden bowls with wooden spoons
by pinch and dash, past twilight
as if Edison had not been born.

Her modest dress of flowered print
ankle low under full apron,
opaque hose in sturdy black heels
in the simple kitchen where she reigned.

A quiet woman, never idle,
small even in a child's vision
her stature brave as five sons,
dedicated as brothers Maccabee.

Memory laughs at mere words,
root ingredients: potato & onion,
recipes unable to handwrite goodness.
Who can find a Bubbe like mine?

I still hear sizzle as Bubbe spooned
thin circles into hot oil, smell
rich flavors of poor old-world folk
tastes sociable as sour cream & apple sauce.

At the rear of a row, in that dimly lit kitchen
without granite counters or Cuisinart
she fried *latkes* crisp, darkened in heavy skillets
her hair, pepper & salt like the iron.

Grandchildren rewarded with the un-plated best
with fortified bodies our voices sang,
flames danced, dreidels spun
renewing freedom's victory.

We shared a Festival of Light.

Chaninah

On feather filled pillows
he reclines easy as evening
crowned by a Cantor's tower
sable hair a castle shadow,
white robe billowing
as if a cumulus cloud.

In sundown sky he presides
minyan of five sons and wives,
stained glass blessings
sweet wine sipped four times,
children on shins a threshold
away, ask why in *four questions*.

Each year on the same full moon
he appears with Elijah, cloaked
in melody at mystery's doorway,
psalms and folksongs
a virtual choir of crystal vibration,
midnight verses accelerando.

Like ten plagues *passing over*
a violent sea split in two, forty years
wandering to a land promised,
this family around that table
on a night different from all others
nothing less than a quiet miracle.

Here I Am
    for Hazzan Leopold Edelstein

Before we heard tears ascend
as melody,
before he ever entered our sanctuary
clad in white,
    he survived
when fear crushed reason

Malicious digits
inked on his forearm,
    severed right hand
replaced by lifeless grip

    He stood silent
bowed at the back wall
head covered, shoulders
draped in humility

It was the *Head of the Year*
our sanctuary full, walls unfolded
like arms open   a congregation
faced forward or heads buzzed to neighbors,

He inhaled, then in motion
began slowly, chanting: *Hineni*
    Here I Am
ready as Abraham to sacrifice
as Moses to serve

Toward the holy ark
he ascended East,
    one voice
    pleading

for prayers to be pleasing

sincere hearts cleansed
as though sin had never been

roots

below the sigh of barren branches
a duvet of dried leaves lie

where we plant our dear departed
grounded in eternal night

at home with bones and worms
living anchors like fingers reach

deeper, even after frost hits hard
tempered by Earth's volcanic core

roots enriched by organic decay
extract sacred compost

sustenance as drawn through a straw
rises up the family trunk

every season banks its promise
inherits a precious storehouse

look at the spreading limbs of a tree
flip that upright image upside-down

Ode to a Peach Tree on Oakland Street

You were a long shot
simple seed, dried pit
sown beneath untilled sod
cultivated to plump maturity,
on a plot little more than a table.

On a block settled by kindred strangers
other neighbors planted concrete,
hucksters howled from farm trucks
in the one-way street: *Hey!*
Get yah fresh Jerr-sey produce!

You delivered pastel blossoms
fragrance seductive as an orchard
terraced above asphalt grid,
abundant yields of velvet skinned orbs
luscious as tropical moonlight.

O' Prunus persica, upright you are
magestic as *purple mountains*
freestone under American skies,
our sweet portion of *fruited plain*
a lance leafed beauty, golden jubilee.

Together

French apple pie
warm, mouthwatering
white icing and raisins extra
celebration on my tongue

Coffee, black and hot
beans ground from exotic latitudes
subtle, smoky aroma
caffeine boost

Sip roasted comfort, taste Eden
five chromed chairs round a marbled table
that setting whole, intimate as twilight
fleeting as lifetimes

I cradle a cup of strong brew,
savor a sweet bite
more satisfying than dessert,
coffee breaks call me home

Dad chose French apple
Mom loved coffee, lightened
with condensed milk—
for 63 years the perfect pair

Unfenced Evenings

Mom, when I speak with you
you are not tucked in your place
as if fetal
in a velvet womb, and I am
not the little boy tucked close.

Like Western silhouette, melting
together in blood sun,
we watched with equal zeal
toughness & tenderness
of *The Rifleman*.

We admired piercing blue eyes
taut leathered skin
on his 6' 5" cowboy frame,
war veteran, father, widower
at planked edge of sagebrush.

Unlike that lone Pa on the frontier
you faced a partner in our clay house
not deadly outlaws on a dusty street.
Your hands, not rawhide rough
never gripped a Winchester.

I recall you giving and giving
constant as boundless prairie,
willing to take a bullet
like *Lucas McCain* for his son,
fearless, and selfless.

You guided me, confident
as the moon rising
ambitions cloudless in cobalt dusk,
like our TV hero, unafraid
bowed but to justice.

December 26, 1960

My 14th birthday
Early morning 18 degrees, clearing skies
We entered Camac Baths from the alley near 12th and Walnut
Front door conspicuous as a speakeasy
The *shvitz* with Dad and Uncle Shim, diminutive for *Shimon*
Clothes hung in metal lockers, keys hung around necks
Winter skin dressed for sports or undressed for loose fit
Raquetball and skinny-dipping in the painted brick basement
Sips of icewater served every 10 minutes in parched heat
In the steam room, river rocks ladled from Schuylkill River tap
Pine scent not reminiscent of forest after morning rain
Fluttering like a ballerina, landing like a bear
Russian masseur, *plaitza* slaps, marble slabs
Tender oak leaves bundled to a soapy broom
Pleasures of the frozen old country, citizens in the new
Paunchy patrons draped in sheets like Roman Senators
Cigar smoke wafted across corned beef specials on rye
Vanilla egg cream fresh from the fountain, no eggs or cream
Monday, December 26, 1960
One year after my ceremonial admission to the tribe
Seven seasons before Super Bowl became America's grail
Football waited 'til Monday, the day *after* Christmas
From folding chairs, testosterone shouted at a 21-inch tube
One smooth face among stubbled Caesars in a deli colosseum
At sold out Franklin Field: Philadelphia 17—Green Bay 13
The Eagles, our beloved *Birds*, won the NFL championship
My best birthday gift
Three men at the *shvitz*
No batteries required

A Time to Every Purpose

Myrtle, willow, date palm, etrog
gathered together, Sukkot pilgrims
wave thanksgiving: *hosha na! hosha na!*

Cold War harvest, Cuban missiles.
That winter, accordion walls opened
as overture to afternoons, to rows
of skinny kids who gripped racquets,
skipped like fleas, stroked in slow sweeps,
balls strictly *verboten*. Mr. Baack,
5'6" sergeant of court choreography,
his muscled frame on a tall platform
commands like square dance master:
*two steps right, backhand;
one step back, forehand.*

Tennis lessons interrupted,
bursts of six position squat thrusts
to work legs for deuce matches
or wilting price for basketballs,
rebellion when Mr. Baack left the gym.

Thaw to a season of *fragrant vines,*
the voice of doves on mild breezes,
each player allowed one ball,
varsity ambition. Strokes perfected
against a wall while Mr. Baack pranced
inspecting his steadfast apprentices.

Try-outs, Tuesday, April 9th.
Date posted, no exceptions!
Nine made the high school team,
but many that sacred day of Passover
chose Moses, rituals, the ancestral team.

The time of singing is come, lo'
centuries of blood libel, lessons
of past winters never *over and gone.*

Coming of Age

Late afternoon, idled in his stuffed chair
Dad handed me the keys to *the USA*.
1956 Chevrolet in our garage grotto

two-toned like fashionable footwear
of a prior era, boxed in Mom's closet.
One floor below kitchen linoleum

four felt strips on cinder walls defended
pristine doors of India Ivory/Sherwood Green.
That coarse cavern too narrow to contain

middle class success or wheelbase of Dad's
1965 Catalina. Moored like a sleek yacht
at the Oakland Street curb, blue steel glittered,

Aunt Frances tied a red ribbon to the rear-view
mirror. My two-wheeled childhood handed down,
Huffy Convertible saved from Tuesday's trash,

bubble-gum cards thumping against spokes,
streamers patriotic. From the Chevy's tailpipe
smoke rose white, not joyous as a new Pope,

but five bucks filled the tank, 170 horses raced.
Teen glee topped Pontiac pride. My steady girl
snuggled with me on spacious seats, leafy green

canopy of Pennypack Park turned illicit amber
glow of *Little City*. A mounted officer woke us,
he and horse both with toothy grins.

Bashert

Random chances
choices intended
strike us in dreams
or hindsight's slant.

We find each other
following an unworn path
without compass or constellations
like needle in haystack,

one

        in a million,

in a sequence of coincidences
at that starry intersection,

where unlikely meets unbelieveable.

Firstborn

That afternoon her doctor predicted two weeks.
We strolled Victorian hills through unspoiled snow.

Woman's cadence on rocking chair night,
five-minute intervals timed to her womb.

Too embarrassed to call while dawn sleeps,
we go as morning yawns. She forgoes the suitcase.

Urgent drive on February's glossy streets
ahead of the rush, days before the leap.

Brilliant indigo skies faultless as new life.
Quiet hopes exhilarating as winter air.

Event expected, date welcomed late.
Painful delivery, perfect arrival.

Moments of worry and wonder, serene
oblivious to irreversible change.

An icy brook chatters its zigzag path
to kiss estuaries at marshgrass edge.

This cloudless day of natural joy.
This first day but one.

Brothers

Send him back, the firstborn demands.
Boys soon play street games, run
   off to colleges four years apart
bunk beds split, room colors change
   engineer & teacher they became.

Brothers closer and closer, if figured
as four is to eight, sixteen to twenty
   not close like a headlock
   or fingers stiff against sternum,
close as a saving hand at ravine's edge.

I remember our single-file trek
   on a narrow ridge, me at the rear
painted cairns ahead in ghostly mist,
   we were moist as dew point
   still wet behind experience.

Atop New Hampshire presidents
   alpine meadows unpaved,
sweaty challenge on switchback paths
   backpack pace, though boys
crave resort happiness not wilderness.

   Ascending Mt. Eisenhower the sky lifts,
humid density spills and they scamper
   up the summit cone beyond sight,
joyful howls carry on wind
   across a four year chasm.

Glaciers carved granite peaks in three states,
vanished valleys boil with clouds
   like blood thick soup,
   every callous or caring act a badge
worn heavy as a backpack or an apology.

Gettysburg

Eight miles north of Mason-Dixon
this peaceful borough and surrounding farms
adorned in summer's riches,
at the crossroads of conflict
boys in uniforms blue and gray
Union and Confederate, converged
under heated skies uncertain
spilling their youth red, on lush green
rolling fields. Barriers of rocks
and sharpened stakes, divided
the postcard landscape
disturbed by uncivil struggle,
blood of brothers seeped into loam,
51,000 broken bodies
tested a nation's endurance.

Millions now visit this hallowed place
peaceful again, to ponder
turning points and dangerous turns
monuments to glory and to loss,
to recite a martyred President's
healing words, while boys, and girls
from Virginia and New York
from Maryland and Pennsylvania,
battle nearby on fields lined white
in uniforms blue and gray
green, and black, and gold,
pursuing goals with breath heated
their instrument, a soccer ball
exploding off a potent foot
deadly as cannon round.

Archaeology

Footprints so close together
we could have been touching

walking hip to hip, arm over
shoulder or holding hands.

These footsteps follow like fossils
facts written in rock, centuries

apart, fragments of bone and pottery
discovered in clay, shards of memory

excavated in deeper layers. The moon
measures each month, years revolve

in grand ellipse around the sun.
Blessings may be burdens and burdens

blessings, a kind of quid pro quo
granted for something done or shunned.

Forty days and forty nights of hard rain,
waters that recede to rainbows,

when a dove with fresh olive branch
finds the living paired like footprints.

Letter to Miss Liberty

Arrived from France, a copper gift of friendship, we placed you on a pedestal with million-dollar views of New York. Boatloads of people wave, take selfies. Everyone looks up to you! You listened to languages, observed men, women & children of every color, changes in dress & attitudes for more than a monumental century. My grandparents never forgot your welcome sight, your *mild eyes*. These days, people fly into Kennedy International, or Newark if you can imagine that. Great winged machines, scream louder than seabirds above your *enlightened* crown, though you do not see runways or borders. No cellphone in your pocket, no Twitter either. Few, favor the tactile folds of news print, but perhaps you read The Times, as commuters & tourists ferry past. Our nation mired in disagreement. The world boiling.

Mother of Exiles, you whose face weathers wars and tides, *beacon* of empathy for *huddled masses yearning to breathe free*, tell us what's happening. You were conceived for the centennial of our Independence, inspired by the struggle against ourselves to *proclaim emancipation*, preserve *a more perfect Union*. Honor General Washington's fight for democracy, General Lafayette's service to that noble cause, a people who *dissolved* a king's tyranny, a young nation that *gave bigotry no sanction, persecution no assistance*. What the hell is happening? It's seventy-five years since American & Allied forces liberated your homeland from fascist boots at Normandy. Please, explain why name calling and stonewalling succeed. Fellow citizens, whose ancestors arrived clothed only in ambition, demand higher walls, more cages. Do you smell the overripe stench of hypocrisy?

Our experiment in self-government continues, each generation debates, inclusive too slowly for those treated as unequals, each vote less grand than the first Congress, *Founding Fathers* who sweated July 4th details in my hometown Philadelphia. Now, articulate discussion is diminished to sound bytes, segregated by cable channels, legislation choked, each side too right to reach reasoned compromise. Yet, Emma's sonnet remains our iconic message, your *flaming torch* a symbol of enduring hope. Have you noticed the water level inching toward your skirt, can you recommend a remedy for pessimism?

Why the Oceans Are Salty

He set jewels, or toilets during Depression,
raised pullies and pipes that rushed ships
from Chester dry docks to war, swam
across the treacherous Delaware on a dare.
He spoke the whole truth without bravado
when important, never self-important
tethered honesty for a salty story.

In a dashing time, long before being born
the second of seven, wooden ships weighted
with crystalline cargo sailed drinkable waters
till a monster devoured men. Like puppets
tossed by wind and waves, their precious stores
dissolved by time and tides into briny seas.
He knew why the oceans are salty.

On the deck of *Serenity*, in locks
raised by plumber's liquid gravity,
steel doors swing open to Panama,
Magellan's *peaceful sea* awaits
across the continental divide, deep
and blue. I see his sunny presence
on Atlantic sands, years sailed away.

Before my head stood above white foam
he taught me to read waves, ready
arms for steady curls in soldiered rows
then, to ride the forward surge. We dove
under breakers, way way out our bodies
floating and falling in fluid rhythm.
He and I both giddy as surfer dudes.

In feet-up heaven, his thick tales wrapped us
like beach towels, we howled at silly jokes
loud as the man hawking: *Ice Cream & Ices!*
Most days Uncle Shim schlepped porcelain
up city steps, after dark scrubbed husky hands
with grit. A tea bag took the chill off February.
Simple things made him smile.

Believe
for grandkids, and all that keeps us young

They rolled a snowball gently
  down a gentle mound,
Its size grew ten times quickly
  shape completely round.

Twice more up, they ran to start
  down the wintry pack,
Three white orbs of perfect art
  Daddy helped to stack.

To resemble you and me
  Eli formed a face,
Twig and bark for eyes and mouth
  did he smartly place.

Hannah, ahead of the game
  fitted scarf and hat,
She named their new friend, *Laura*
  Frosty, surely not.

Cole leaped on his Flyer sled
  head down, unaware,
On collision course he sped
  Laura standing there.

Hannah screamed at Cole to stop
  sadly, late to brake,
Laura with the quickstep hop
  real breath did she take?

Frozen still as a sculpture
  Daddy missed her move,
Children will believe wonders
  impossible to prove.

On a clear and moonlit night
  out your window view,
When Winter sparkles just right
  Laura winks at you.

Knock Knock

Who's there?
Kids, little kids.

Little kids who?
Who stand on their toes
head below the line at carnival rides
eager to race time.

Who awake in the sleepy morning
like a tornado in Kansas,
then wobble away
leaving us in the calm eye.

Who squeal and whirl
laughing, leaping, loving
with hysterical zeal,

their song and dance
totally appealing, until
like candy bars left in summer sun
they melt into naps or snacks.

Who plead to hug Elmo
again, and again
or hug the back of your knee,

to avoid eye contact
with the BIG red monster,
their personalities somehow present
from the womb.

Who show and tell in high pitched voices
incapable of woven deception,
gooey as s'mores
around an ageless fire.

Lost and Found

The old high school stood silent
without understanding
what is lost, or found.

Hallways left to metal sentinels
paper shrines scattered, stair towers
once climbed two steps at a time
absent heartbeats.

Listen! Young voices, big dreams
seventy-five years echo
in shadows and dust,
hormones louder than lessons.

Beloved mother forsaken
her face disfigured, sold
to weeds and boarded windows.

The slate lady pushed down
marble and brass salvaged.
School Lane lost its namesake
the town mourns her form.

The muscular new high school
commands fields once corn,
her facade found on the horizon
gift boxes ribboned in brick.

This singular summer—ode and fanfare
melancholy and jubilant each measure.
Teachers, students look over a shoulder,
in procession of circumstance.

Families shout from grandstands
seniors flip tassels, toss hats
into sapphire sky on a June evening.
Nightfall, commences the incoming era.

Another diamond jubilee will come
like lightning through this valley,
thirty thousand fresh faces
competing in a global community.

In the turbine spin of dizzy change
public debates repeat
two-minute intelligence, self-interest
dismissed to yellowed files.

Swift athletes, prom elegance,
hand-shaped pottery and poems
still quicken hearts. Choir and band
harmonize with cafeteria chatter.

In Physics lab, hypnotic pendulum
swings to gravity's pull, youth pushes
limits lost in their wireless world.

Friends and mentors find each other
learning illuminates curiosity,
ideas stream like daylight
through classroom glass.

Lament is lost. Success
invests in common good
in steel and knowledge
in generations who invent the future.

We understand what is lost, and found.

What Would You Write?

What would you write about someone who memorized poems in grade school and recites those verses at 92? Born youngest of five boys, don't dare call him *kid brother,* as he detested that label. Write of his affection for musical theatre, clever libretto. You could praise career change, if Lerner had not met Loewe, Hammerstein not joined Rodgers. Tell of Mario Lanza walking down 6th Street to rehearse or soothe vocal chords with chicken soup. If only the house had space, the family savings for a piano.

What language would be most precise? About someone who grew up speaking Yiddish, singing Hebrew, talking with cats. He studied French, served his country at the Iron Curtain, travelled with Michelin & Alpha Romeo, all before you finished the sixth grade. He heard Roosevelt & Churchill on radio, Chamberlain & Russell hurtle on hardwoods, championships announced in Zinkoff's smooth baritone. Carry on conversations with *the Lord* or *the Stilt,* speculations about basketball or geopolitics. One on one, game faces on. With wine or whiskey, without cigars.

Who will your narrative recall or imagine? The boy who caught footballs on city playgrounds. A man in dark blue, fedora and overcoat, suited to hop the train to UN headquarters. Someone who admired Moe Berg, trained with firearms & secrets, investigated mobsters and corruption in cities from Miami to Chicago. Familiar with the drive to DC, be clear he would volunteer for the special counsel's team, audit transactions & taxes, conduct interviews with calculator & intelligence.

What was, is, or could be? Truth, not cold facts or eulogy. Score matches on grass courts in short whites, when season and elbow allow. Describe brunch at the nineteenth century cricket club. Quote more exclusive *gentlemen* born twenty years earlier, who did not permit *his kind* to join. In that alternate chronology, he'd be living closer to Krakow than Philadelphia. Love Uncle Dave's stories, gifts to his brothers' children, children & grandchildren of those nieces & nephews. A son attentive to his mother. Use chosen words, a clean handkerchief. Name this man, name him. Keen observer, suspicious of power, conscious of history rhyming.

For Your Sore Throat

Don't gargle, Google *guggle muggle*
before dismissing it as mere gibberish
like verse read *Through the Looking-Glass*
or that *super* silly word Mary Poppins sings.

Served in a cup with handle, it's not British slang
like J.K. Rowling's adapted label for a foolish class.
Not New Orleans roaring 20's colloquial for cannabis,
nor does it swim with genus *mugil*, of Latin lexicon.

Search alternate spellings, hyphenated or not,
counted as accents of Eastern Europe. I prefer
gogl mogl (in glass, please), though etymology
favors no transliteration, articulates no meaning.

Depending where your mother or grandmother
was born, you may know this remedy, ingredients
available in deepest winter when most needed,
more soothing than echinacea or chicken soup.

Rocky's 4 AM protein breakfast powered his body
through Philly streets, up those Parkway steps—
only partial prescription. Ask Barbra Streisand
her singer's secret to nourish vocal apparatus.

Whisk raw eggs into honey sweet warm milk,
this foaming dessert, vanilla or cinnamon flavored
(to your taste). On bitter mornings watch Poppy
add a shot of slivovitz when Mom's not looking.

Fairy Dust

Shhh! Sister & I on pajama fours
pillows snug as our secret. Eyes giggle
heads touch, ears listen at the air duct
for grown-up talk, curious to stay up late.

Not satisfied with mumbled voices
we take turns on tummies, hands on ankles
bodies dangle headfirst down steps
peeking without permission.

Now, busy on opposite coasts, decades
flash like shooting stars. Sister & I
wish upon each flickering year. Eyes
giggle, heads touch on rare summer nights.

Roles reversed, we coach words
bending level with childrens' eyes,
or dangle their legs from our shoulders
pretending, sprinkled with fairy dust.

We blow away birthdays, surrender
to ephemeral youth, ride rollercoasters
hands in air, bodies braced through tight turns
screaming at the steep descent.

Promise and memory fly together
carefree as balloons on a string.

How Do I Know You?

Bliss faded like paper flowers
   with her body   his mind
sometimes he forgot she was gone

He needed to hear all was well
before his head tilted   asleep
missing her goodnight kiss

He aimed a tin arrowhead
at letters   twenty-six flip-up lists
meticulous narration in thin ink
lifeline to a lifetime

One by one he dialed mechanically
asked casually: *How do I know you?*
   sundown   short talks repeated
his minutes as breath in cold air

He could chant hymns & haftorahs
name every street north of Oregon Avenue
did not remember   colors of October

When he confused nights with days
cousins from area codes circled
   I took his address book
guilty as a disobedient child

Names and numbers engraved
   in granite at King David's Cemetery
rows like empty seats in the sanctuary
   missing his tenor voice

Guessing Game

She predicted death by her 60th birthday
hers before mine, stating without sorrow
evidence against actuaries: *I am
my oldest living relative.*

Her reality reflects this orphan's history:
tumors took Mom at 57 years, Dad at 46
neither leaving siblings, half-uncles
metastasized by indifference.

Her demise predicted, then diagnosed:
lymphatic signature, fair-skinned kin
to melanoma, cousin to lumpectomy,
chemo and radiation the toxic protocol.

A decade past her three-score bet
she sings: *Sha—la—la la la la*
living without excuse for today's excess
a hummingbird hovering near sugar.

Her pleasures, shopping treasures:
bunnies in pleats, snowmen in smiles,
pastel seashells, pumpkins aplenty;
each wrapped or unwrapped in its season.

If I lay in a king bed without my queen
a queen who acts a princess,
should I care which bare season is here
or next, would trees burst with color?

She likes to play a guessing game
testing my notice of her latest *tchotchke*.
I could not play if monarchs and angels stare,
her winged persona relentless as the calendar.

No! Let me be the first to die
to mourn not, to grieve no loss.
Let me also sing: *Sha—la—la la la la,*
unbound witness to her cup running over.

Prayer

Unspoken pleas rise above rooftops
buoyant on hope's thermal air,

ardent messages heard, ears cupped
in heaven's contented abode.

We toss and turn through restless nights
lost in a labyrinth of questions, aware

of searching light as it angles away,
inspiration but a waning moment.

In morning's fair countenance, informed
by fact & belief, compassion & fear,

in minds, in matter, hit or miss,
what touches a human heart?

Remember those resonant pleas,
moonless desires, dreamlike replies,

the brilliant flash of blinding truth
before dawn lifted her silver veil.

Who can say when prayer is answered,
why will things be as they will be?

DeLorean Flight

Sepia poses stand
on Bubbe's sideboard
like a rear-view mirror,
undiscovered futures
rush to be present.

We are time travelers
exceeding light speed,
hurled at synaptic pace
to nostalgic places
or anxious corners.

Signposts disappear
in clouds of routine
noted ahead, reflecting
back. Earth spins
without thought or stop.

Clocks and galaxies orbit,
grains in an hourglass
pile on the past. None
possess nor hold time
still, in our palm.

We hurry or hesitate, hopeful
good things will come
while patience waits, but
time is not on your side or mine,
no, it's not, no it's not.

Notes

Epigram: English translation from "The Jewish Study Bible", by Jewish Publication Society, Oxford University Press, Inc. (2004)

"L'dor Vador": In liturgy, refers to "continuity, passing on spiritual knowledge, sustaining heritage, collective memory."(Milken Archive)
1. *shande* (shame or scandal), *shtetls* (villages), *Bubbie* (grandmother), *Zayda* (grandfather), *shmaltzed* (enriched) chicken fat or sentimentality.
2. *Israel* (Genesis 32:25—29), original name Jacob, father of 12 tribes.

"Poppy": Maternal grandfather, Reuben Mazer, immigrant from Kiev, came to US in 1905. My roommate growing up in NE Philly.
1. *golden land*, from optimistic Yiddish expression, *goldene medina*

"Sophie": Maternal grandmother, passed away in 1946, at 62 years. Poppy lived another 19 years, but never remarried.
1. *kvell*—to express great pride. Cognate of German, *quellen*, to swell
2. "covenant"—*bris*, circumcision/ naming ceremony (Genesis 17:10—12)
3. *Shprintze, Peretz*—My father crafted my Hebrew name with three letters from her Yiddish name: *Pey*—פ; *Resh*—ר; *Tzade*—צ.

"1521 Dickinson Street": Small business in Italian neighborhood. Poppy joked, too many tailors east of Broad. Sewing machine on exhibit, National Museum of American Jewish History on Independence Mall.

"Anna": Paternal grandmother. Only grandparent at our wedding.
1. *Who can find...?* See Proverbs (31:10), "Woman of valour..."
2. *latkes,* potato pancakes. Unknown oil, perhaps her secret ingredient
3. We played betting game with *dreidel*, a spinning top, winning walnuts

"Chaninah": Paternal grandfather, Charles Issac Pollack, known by his Hebrew name, Cantor in South Philly *shuls*. Passover Seder, he led, perhaps my earliest memory. He died before my 7th birthday.
1. *minyan,* quorum of ten adults
2. *four questions, four sips of wine, Elijah* (prophet), *ten plagues,* rituals in "Haggadah", book which narrates the Exodus from Egypt.

"Here I Am": Leopold Edelstein (1909—1985), prayer leader and choir director at Beth Emeth Congregation in 1950's. Born in Czechoslovakia, his prosthetic hand told of Holocaust horrors. His expressive voice, theatrical flair and love of Jewish music nurtured that joy in me.

1. "*Hineni*", known as the Cantor's prayer. Practical plea. Hebrew word implies both a physical and spiritual readiness
2. Word spoken by Abraham (Gen. 22:1) when asked to sacrifice his son, by Moses (Exodus 3:4) upon seeing a bush burning, not consumed

"**Ode to a Peach Tree**": *purple mountain majesties, fruited plain*—from poem "America the Beautiful" by Katharine Lee Bates (1859—1929)

"**Unfenced**": *Rifleman*, TV Western (1958—1963). Chuck Connors, athlete turned actor, who starred as Lucas McCain, broke cultural ground as widowed Dad raising his son. His distinctive rifle a last resort.

"**December 26, 1960**":
1. *shvitz*, literally to sweat, a sauna or steam bath
2. *plaitza*, Yiddish for shoulders and back, massage technique

"**A Time to Every Purpose**": title from Ecclesiastes 3:1
1. Sukkot—autumn harvest festival, literally "booths", temporary structures (Lev 23:33—42) *Myrtle, willow, etc*—products of the land.
2. *hosha na*—Hebrew, "save us", chanted while waving branches.
3. *fragrant vines, doves, time of singing*—(Song of Songs 2:11—13)
4. Passover—spring festival of freedom (Exodus 12:14—20)
5. blood libel—false allegations spread throughout Europe in Middle Ages (by Nazis in 20th century), that Jews used blood of murdered Christian children in Passover rituals.

"**Coming of Age**":
1. *the USA*. "See the U SA in your Chevrolet...". Sponsor's song, signature of Dinah Shore on her weekly TV variety show.
2. *Huffy Convertible,* childrens bicycle by Huffy Corp, Dayton, Ohio.
3. *Little City,* "make-out" spot, lover's lane popular with teenagers, off Rhawn Street in 1600-acre Pennypack Park.

"**Bashert**": Yiddish, "meant to be", most commonly finding a partner, a "soulmate". More broadly, "fate or destiny".

"**Gettysburg**": *tested a nation's endurance*—Abraham Lincoln's profound 1863 address, delivered at cemetery dedication, the Civil War still raging

"**Letter to Miss Liberty**":
1. phrases from "New Colossus", Emma Lazarus (1849—1887), her iconic sonnet raised money for the pedestal erected in 1886.
2. *Bigotry no sanction, persecution no assistance...* letter written by George

Washington to the Jewish synagogue in Newport, RI in 1790

"Archaeology": *forty days and forty nights, rainbow, dove with olive branch*; references to Biblical Noah's ark (Genesis 7—9).

"Why the Oceans are Salty": Uncle Shim, Simon Frank, worked at Sun Shipyards in Chester, PA during WWII. After the war, he started a plumbing/heating business with his oldest brother.
1. Crystal Serenity, cruise ship, passing through the Panama Canal.
2. *peaceful sea*—Magellan named the Pacific Ocean, "undiscovered" body of water, as he circumnavigated the globe.

"Lost and Found": Reflection on 8 years of planning, public hearings, government approvals, design/construction of Souderton Area High School occupied in Sept 2009. 445,000 sq foot building on 105 acres.

"What Would You Write?":
1. Dave Zinkoff (1910—1985) P.A. announcer. Philly sports fixture.
2. Morris (Moe) Berg (1902—1972). Major league catcher, Princeton and Columbia Law, spoke several languages, gathered intelligence behind Nazi lines during WWII.
3. "cricket club", historic Germantown (1854—present).
his kind, gentlemen—many private institutions excluded Jews, African Americans, other minorities during their long history.
4. "history rhyming"—The quote: "History does not repeat itself, but often rhymes", attributed to Mark Twain. Greek concept.

"Guessing Game":
1. "Let's Live for Today", song by David Shapiro, lyrics Michael Julien. Rock band, Grass Roots, made the song a hit in 1967:
> When I think of all the worries
> People seem to find
> And how they're in a hurry
> To complicate their minds...
> Sha-la-la-la-la-la, live for today
2. *tchotchke*, a small trinket, decorative rather than functional
3. *cup running over*, from Psalm 23

"DeLorean Flight": *time is not on your side or mine*, twist on the song written by Jerry Ragovoy, "Time Is on My Side". Made popular by the Rolling Stones recording in 1964.

Steve Pollack was born nine months and two weeks after his father was discharged from the US Army at the end of WWII. He grew up in NE Philly, attended local public schools and community religious schools. He graduated from Drexel University in 1969, a Mechanical Engineer. He worked as a student and later, a civilian professional for the US Navy. He moved southwest to experience life on the other side of the Mississippi and to work his right brain. He graduated from the University of Texas at Austin in 1973, an MS in Community and Regional Planning.

He's been an usher, delivery boy, drug crisis volunteer, engineer, project manager and administrator. Over a 40 year career, he was employed by governmental and non-profit organizations including the PA Department of Community Affairs, Philadelphia Office of Housing and Community Development, Warminster Heights Development Corp, Fox Chase Cancer Center and Souderton Area School District. Following completion of a new high school in 2009, he retired as Supervisor of Planning and Operations (call him "free agent"). He attended too many meetings. Never owned a minor league baseball team.

His short story about a snowman was published in the "Chronicle", the annual literary magazine of Solis Cohen Elementary School. His career focused writing skills for technical or advocacy purposes. He found poetry (or poetry found him) later. He enjoys the precision and sound of language, the creative process, even revisions. Some of his individual poems have been published in anthologies. That makes him feel good. This is his first chapbook. He volunteers on advisory boards for the Montgomery County Poet Laureate Program and One Book One Jewish Community. He sings bass with Nashirah, the Jewish Chorale of Greater Philadelphia and with Tiferet Bet Israel choir on High Holidays.

He and Linda live in Woxall, PA, near chickens and horses. They met at her best friend's sweet sixteen party on Rutland Street in 1964 and have been *going steady* ever since. They celebrated their 50th wedding anniversary on November 2, 2019, blessed with two sons, their lovely wives and four grandchildren.

woxallsteve@gmail.com

www.ingramcontent.com/pod-product-compliance
Lightning Source LLC
LaVergne TN
LVHW041555070426
835507LV00011B/1102